The Traveller's Little Instruction Book

I thought this little book
would come in handy!

With all my love
Jennifer
x x

Also available from Thorsons

A BABY'S LITTLE INSTRUCTION BOOK
David Brawn
A CAT'S LITTLE INSTRUCTION BOOK
Leigh W. Rutledge
A DOG'S LITTLE INSTRUCTION BOOK
David Brawn
THE DRIVER'S LITTLE INSTRUCTION BOOK
Mike Leonard
LIFE'S LITTLE INSTRUCTION BOOK
H. Jackson Brown Jr.
LIFE'S LITTLE INSTRUCTION BOOK, VOLUME II
H. Jackson Brown Jr.
THE LOVERS' LITTLE INSTRUCTION BOOK
Cindy Francis
THE OFFICE LIFE LITTLE INSTRUCTION BOOK
Holly Budd
THE PARENT'S LITTLE INSTRUCTION BOOK
Cindy Francis
A TEDDY BEAR'S LITTLE INSTRUCTION BOOK
David and Tracey Brawn

The Traveller's Little Instruction Book

Jo Kyle & Meg Slyfield

Thorsons
An Imprint of HarperCollins*Publishers*

Thorsons
An Imprint of HarperCollins*Publishers*
77– 85 Fulham Palace Road,
Hammersmith, London W6 8JB
1160 Battery Street
San Francisco, California 94111–1213

Published by Thorsons 1996
1 3 5 7 9 10 8 6 4 2

© Jo Kyle and Meg Slyfield 1996

Jo Kyle and Meg Slyfield assert the moral right to
be identified as the authors of this book

A catalogue record for this book
is available from the British Library

ISBN 0 7225 3235 0

Cartoons by Gray Jolliffe

Printed in Great Britain by
HarperCollinsManufacturing Glasgow

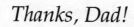

Thanks, Dad!

Introduction

Travelling is not simply about getting from A to B. Oh no, there's far more too it than that! It's about everything that goes before, during and after ... the pre-departure stress, the post-arrival excitement and the inevitable post-mortem.

It's about trying to catch a plane from Heathrow when you should be at Gatwick; it's about unfriendly customs officials who *always* seem to pick on you when you have a suitcase full of dirty knickers; it's about the seductive smell of suntan lotion ... and the pain of sunburn; it's about the pleasure of sipping daiquiris on the beach and *Glühwein* in the mountains; it's about losing your inhibitions on exotic islands and being eternally grateful that you're not like this back home; it's about trying to keep your cool on a 10-hour bus journey even though you're suffering from chronic 'Delhi belly' – and it's about those holiday snaps that didn't quite come out as expected.

So, all you globe-trotters out there, read these tips ... and keep on moving!

☀ Smile, you're going on holiday

☀ Try not to look too smug – you'll only lose friends

☼ Beware of grinning travel agents.
They don't fancy you – they're just
thinking of their hefty commission

☼ Don't let them wax lyrical about a 'hot'
resort – it's probably still a building site

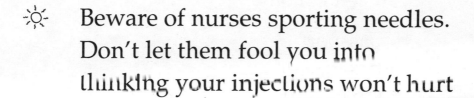 Beware of nurses sporting needles. Don't let them fool you into thinking your injections won't hurt

Make sure none of the following are left at home:

- passport
- ticket
- credit card
- young son

☼   If you plan to travel with someone, take a compatible person

☼   If you plan to travel alone, take a good book, Walkman, cards for solitaire, attitude...

☼ Don't rely on your holiday to revive
your sex life ... especially if you are
sharing a room with the kids

☼ Don't expect to get handcuffs and
whips through customs without
comment

Survival tips for backpackers:

- Fill your rucksack, then divide the contents by a third
- Take plenty of money to buy everything you left behind
- A money belt may be uncomfortable, but not half as uncomfortable as sleeping on the street

- ☼ Don't criticize anyone who drives you to the airport – they might not come back to pick you up

- ☼ Toy guns are not ideal presents to take with you

☀ If you want to get upgraded on a flight, arrive early, look businesslike and smile a lot

☀ If the flight is overbooked, be loud and obnoxious

- ☼ Accept that you will always choose the slowest check-in queue

- ☼ Avoid aisle seats when other passengers are on the run

- ☼ Book an aisle seat if you're on the run

☼ Confuse passport officials by looking nothing like your photo

☼ If you do look like your photo, you are not well enough to travel

☼ Accept that you will never sit next to anyone interesting on a plane

☼ Accept that you will always sit next to the crying baby

☼ Never open up a conversation with a dull-looking neighbour on a long flight – there is no escape

☼ If a dull neighbour starts to get chatty with you, remind them of some great disaster movies

☼ Before slipping off your shoes on the plane, try to remember whether you had time to change your socks this morning

☼ Don't crick your neck trying to locate the drinks trolley coming up the aisle – it won't have started yet

☼ Don't eat too many peanuts during the flight – you'll only feel sick

☼ When eating your meal, remember to take the plastic cover off. It will taste the same, but it's better for you

☼ Hold on tight to your dinner during a turbulent flight

☼ Don't forget the apologetic smile when you pass the flight attendant your bulging sick bag

☼ It is not a good idea to take sick leave and spend it on the beach in the Caribbean

☼ Sitting behind the tallest passenger does nothing to enhance your enjoyment of the film

☼ Being the tallest passenger does nothing to enhance your enjoyment of the flight

☼   You should have known it was a mistake to see that film last week

☼   The film you hoped to see is bound to be showing in first class

☀ On a night flight, accept that no one but you will have problems sleeping in an upright chair with no leg room

☀ After two sleepless hours, don't let your neighbour's snoring get you down

☼ After four sleepless hours, resist throttling your snoring neighbour

☼ After six sleepless hours, expect a flight attendant to wake you with a cold face towel just as you nod off

Don't let your neighbour using his face towel to wipe his armpits put you off your breakfast

☼ Restrain your in-flight neighbour from standing up too quickly and knocking red wine into your lap

☼ Don't wear stilettos when flying – your feet will swell and you totter enough as it is

Survival tips for recession-hit business travellers:

- Ask your chairman if you can fly first class
- Ask your chairman if you can fly business class
- Be happy to fly economy
- Pray none of your competitors are on the same flight in first or business class

☼ Accept that your case will always be last onto the baggage reclaim

☼ Keep your cool when you are the only person left waiting – your Bermuda shorts might not have been redirected to Bermuda

☼ If you help a little old lady with her bags off the carousel, don't be surprised if she has lots of friends appearing from nowhere

☼ Expect your luggage trolley to always be moving towards a different destination than you

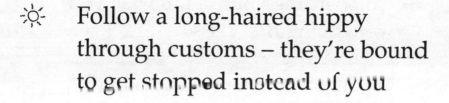

☼   Follow a long-haired hippy through customs – they're bound to get stopped instead of you

☼   This plan is not foolproof!

☼ On boarding your flight, wish you were flying first class

☼ On arrival, feel relieved you didn't waste your money

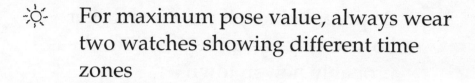

☼ For maximum pose value, always wear two watches showing different time zones

☼ When asked the time, say, 'Of course that depends...'

-☼- Be prepared to tell your taxi driver how to reach your destination – he is probably new in town

-☼- When on foot, assume every driver is a maniac

- ☼ Hire a convertible at least once in your life

- ☼ Crunching gears and macho hand-brake spins are always more fun if it's not your car

Survival tips for skiers:

- Remember that your ski instructor is not God
- Wear your bobble hat and scarf with pride
- Convince yourself it's character building to be stuck on a chair lift in a blizzard

-☼- If you are on a budget, treat yourself to at least one night in a luxury hotel

-☼- Fill your washbag with all the toiletries from the bathroom

-☼- Leave the towels – they'll charge you

Survival tips for package holidays:

- Expect your transfer bus to acquaint you with every hotel in the resort before yours
- Remember your hotel will look nothing like it does in the brochure
- Complain to your rep
- Remind yourself at least it was cheap

-☼-   Try and relax

-☼-   Wish you'd left the kids at home

☼   Annoy other tourists by putting your towel out on the sun-lounger the night before

☼   Be considerate – keep fellow guests cool by dive bombing into the pool

☼ Don't try to pee surreptitiously in the swimming-pool. It may react with chemicals in the water to form a brightly coloured cloud.

☼ If this happens, glare at a nearby child.

☼ Always lie next to someone fatter than you on the beach

☼ Always lie next to someone whiter than you on the beach

Fashion tips for women:

- Try on your swimsuit in the privacy of your own bedroom before making an embarrassing mistake on a crowded beach
- Bikinis are only for the young and firm
- That ethnic dress won't look the same once you get home

☼ If you are suddenly surrounded by a group of animated men, stop sunbathing topless

☼ Apply suntan lotion before you burn, not after

☼ Shake out the sand in your towel just as your neighbour slaps on another layer of suntan cream

☼ Don't be too disappointed – lifeguards tend not be as well endowed in real life as on *Baywatch*

- ☼ If you are single, enjoy sneering at couples walking hand in hand along the beach

- ☼ If you are a couple, flaunt your status in the sunset

☼ Watch *From Here to Eternity*, then frolic in the waves with your partner

☼ Watch out when having sex on the beach – the sand might rupture your condom

☼ Stop wearing aftershave if the only things you are attracting are mosquitoes

☼ Provide beach entertainment by singing along to your Walkman

☼ Give this a miss if you are listening to Barry Manilow

☼ Unwind in the sun – but don't unravel

☼ Don't rent a pedalo by yourself –
you'll end up going round in circles

☼   Remember a suntan lasts a couple of weeks ... wrinkles last a lifetime

☼   Don't forget your bald patch when slapping on the suncream

☼ If red is not your colour, don't spend 10 hours in the sun on the first day

☼ If grey is not your colour, leave those white t shirts at home

☼ If green is not your colour, don't ask others how much longer they've got left

☀ Don't mock your dad's shorts –
yours may look just as stupid

☀ Don't wear skimpy swimming trunks
if you're well endowed – you could
cause offence

Lie in the shade of a coconut tree

 Ponder Newton's Law of Gravity

 Move under a parasol – it's safer

If a sunbronzed god/goddess offers to oil your back, make sure you've got a full bottle

☼ Remember that the Dead Sea is a great beach holiday for the non-swimmer

☼ Never trust a Spanish waiter – his trousers are too tight and his previous conquests too close together

☼ If you must relieve yourself in the sea, have the grace to swim around a bit

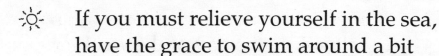 Avoid a holiday in the monsoon season – it's bound to be a washout

☼ Lose track of the day of the week

☼ Make sure you watch the sunrise at least once

☼   A sense of humour will take you far

  Don't lose your head over lost
sunglasses – they're probably on it

Survival tips for boats:

- Ginger capsules are a great natural preventative for motion sickness
- Remember not to chew them before swallowing
- If they fail, go on deck and scan the horizon
- Before being sick, check which way the wind is blowing

☼ When in India, don't complain that you can get a better curry from your local Balti house

☼ When in China, don't complain that you can get a better sweet 'n' sour from your local take-away

☼　　When in Thailand, don't complain that you can get better chicken satay sticks from your local supermarket

☼　　When in a Spanish resort, expect to get better fish 'n' chips than you do back home

☀ Lose your inhibitions on a Greek island

☀ Your worst chat-up lines often work on holiday

☀ Before you sleep with a stranger, see them sober and by daylight

Essential tips for postcards:

- Annoy others by writing 'wish you were here' on all your postcards
- Send one to your bank manager
- Give this a miss if you're going for broke in Las Vegas

- ☼ Go sky diving, white water rafting, bungy jumping...

- ☼ Buy the t-shirt and video to prove it

- ☼ Never do it again

☼ Never let anyone tell you
you are too old

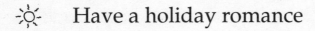 Have a holiday romance

At least you'll have one interesting thing to tell your friends when you get home

☼ If you try to speak the local language, expect to be laughed at

☼ Talking louder won't make people understand you any better

Survival tips for campers:

- Don't think about that luxury hotel room you could have had
- Don't share a one-man tent with a flatulent friend
- Don't share a single sleeping-bag with a lover – only Houdini could make love in something so constrained

☀ Make sure you speak the
language before buying
condoms – if you resort to
a mime, it may cause offence

☼ Take plenty of money for your trip

☼ Do your family really love you enough for that reverse charge call to ask for more cash?

-☼- Boys! Inserting a potato in your trunks will not improve your sex appeal by the pool, even if you do remember to put it at the front

Fashion tips for men:

- Don't expect to be taken seriously when wearing shorts, long socks and open-toed sandals
- Handkerchiefs are not meant to be worn on the head – even if you *are* trying to cover that bald patch
- Brightly coloured shirts serve merely to enhance a middle-age spread

☀   Try to save money when sightseeing

☀   It always pays to tag along on someone else's guided tour

☼ Pose for photos – especially when
you're not meant to be in them

☼ Don't bother to read your guidebook
in advance – you'll never remember
which monument is which

☼ Always pack a condom –
it doubles as an excellent
shower or bathing cap

-☼-　　When meeting foreigners, feel superior by pointing out something about their hometown they didn't know

-☼-　　Hope they haven't visited yours

 See the Seven Wonders of the World

☀ Ask someone what they are

☼ Don't drink water from the Ganges, Nile ... or Thames

☼ Don't dream of luxurious sit-down toilets when there's only a hole in the ground to squat over

Survival tips for Delhi belly:

- Always carry a spare pair of knickers/boxers/y-fronts in case of an accident
- Be grateful that at least you are fit enough to sprint
- Don't be surprised if you're not in the mood for sex

☼ If you are going to miss a train or bus, arrive so late that you don't have long to wait for the next one

☼ Accept that bus and train windows are always stuck open in the winter and glued shut in the summer

-☼- Always exaggerate the size of the spider/cockroach/snake. It makes a much better story

-☼- If you're in a foreign city and feeling homesick, don't panic – there's bound to be a McDonald's round the corner

It is not advisable to breastfeed in a crowded carriage on an Italian train

Survival tips for motorists:

- Always drive on the right side of the road, even if it is the left
- Don't criticize the map reader. Could you really do any better?
- Don't fall asleep, wake up and then ask the driver, 'Are we nearly there?'

☀ If a restaurant is empty, ask yourself why

☀ If you're worried about the food, make sure you know the word for 'toilet'

☀ If you can't find any toilet paper, keep this book close at hand

- ☼ Restrain yourself from eating with a knife and fork in Chinese restaurants

- ☼ If you're having problems with your chopsticks, try using one in each hand

Survival tips for hitch-hikers:

- Keep your massive rucksack and huge friend out of sight until a car actually stops
- Back-seat driving is a no-no
- You may be discriminated against if you have a spider's web tattooed on your face

☀ Be kind to the environment

☀ Leave your mother-in-law at home
when picnicking at a beauty spot

☼   An expedition to the jungle is not
the time to discover you don't like
mosquitoes ... or wild animals

☼   A holiday to the Costa del Sol is not the
time to discover you don't like lager ...
or louts

☼ A trek in the Himalayas is not the time to discover you don't like hills ... or walking

☼ A trip to New York is not the time to discover you don't like shopping ... or heights

☼ 'My round' is understood in any language

☼ Always blame the food for your dodgy stomach – but remember 10 pints of lager can have the same effect

☼ Souvenirs might look good in the shop
– but do you really want a plastic Eiffel
Tower on your mantelpiece?

☼ Reserve any dolls in national costume
for your worst enemy

☼ Be cautious in local markets. You may think you're buying a carpet, but you could actually be selling your girlfriend

☼ When you're told an item is unique, it really means the others are still in the box

☀ Remember fake watches bought in local markets don't come with guarantees

☀ Cultivate friends abroad. It makes for cheaper holidays

☀ Enjoy unlimited free flights by marrying a pilot

☀ Be grateful that you fancy men/women in uniform

☀ Accept that you will be confused by foreign currency

☀ Asking locals to help themselves is asking for trouble

Survival tips for safaris:

- Don't expect to see any wildlife, then you won't be disappointed
- Take a zoom lens just in case
- Don't make a crocodile smile
- The cats might look friendly but it is not advisable to try and cuddle them

- ☼ If you must eat live oysters, expect them to fight back

- ☼ Avoid eating a dozen oysters before your journey home

- ☼ Don't expect anyone to be interested in your holiday snaps

- ☼ Wonder why there are so many boring ones of temples and landscapes

- ☼ Blame them on someone else

☼ Fight the temptation to miss the
last train/plane/bus home

☼ Console yourself by stocking up
on duty free

☼ Accept that the sun always sets on the other side of the plane

☼ Accept that your tan will fade – even before you step off the plane

If you pack your dirty underwear in a suitcase with a faulty catch, prepare for embarrassment

☼ Don't carry your talcum powder through customs in a plastic bag

☼ Remember that customs officers have no sense of humour

☼ Learn to say 'Nothing to declare' with a straight face

☀ Don't be a travel story bore – you'll only lose friends

☀ If your holiday romance says they'll write, don't bother waiting by the letterbox

☀ It's never too early to start planning your next trip

☀ Here's to next time